Magical Notes

Piano Book II

For Absolute Beginners
By Sarah Wanda Topolska Shanfari

Magical Notes

Piano For Absolute Beginners

Arranged and Edited By

Sarah Wanda Topolska Shanfari

Smiling Sun

Ten Little Indians

Wishing Star

Pink Stairs

Colourful Balloons

My Teddy Bear

Andante

B flat

Cuckoo

First Waltz

Figaro

Mozart

Moderato

Mozart was an Austrian composer. He composed his first piece of music at the age of five. He travelled all over Europe performing for royalty.
This is a tune from the opera "The Marriage of Figaro".

F Sharp

Moderato

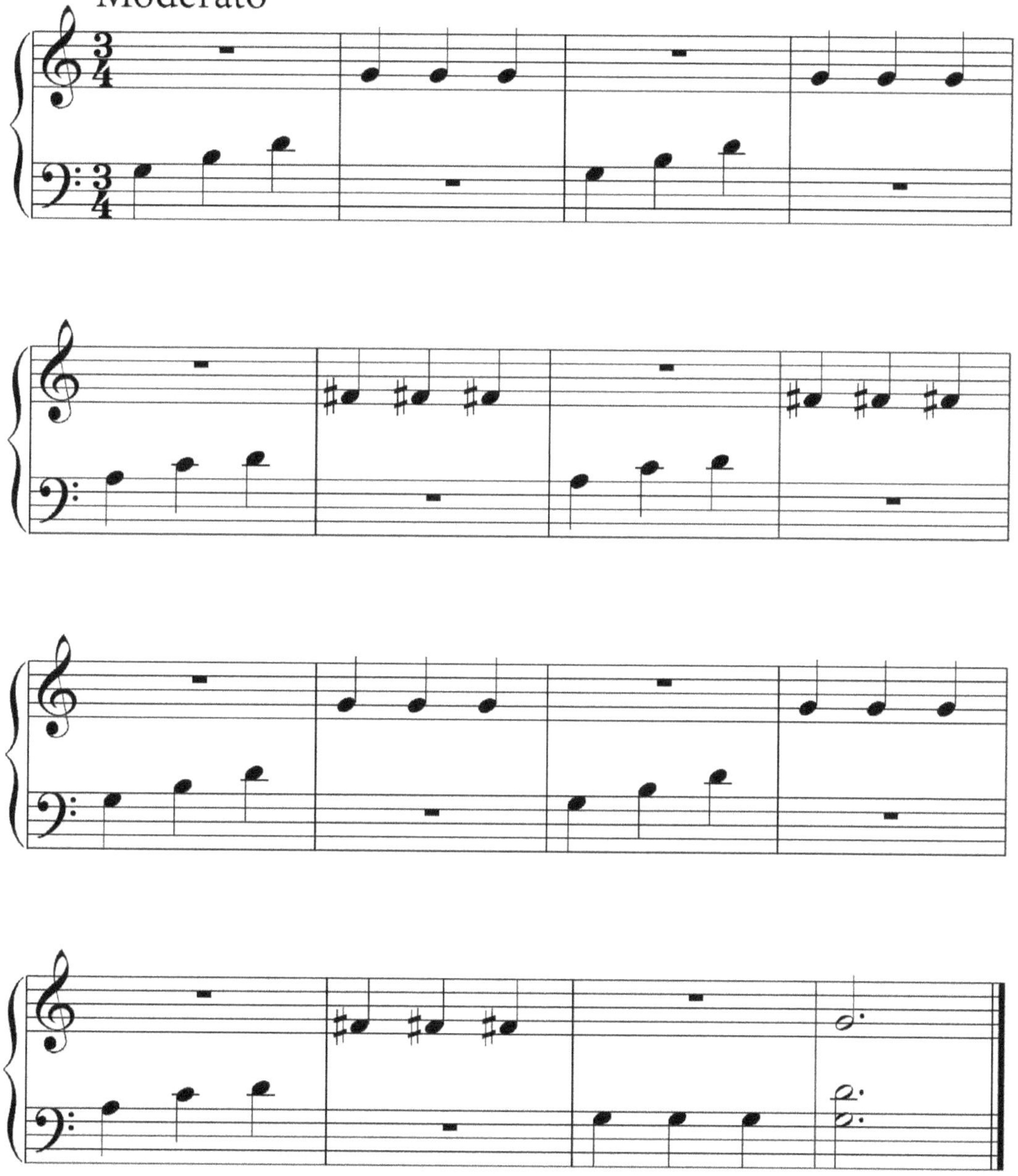

The Whale

Happy Holiday

Little Sonata

Allegro

Clementi

1 finger under

G A B

Clementi was an Italian/English composer. He studied in Rome at an early age.
He loved travelling all around Europe and playing concerts.

London Bridge

Magical Notes

Sarah Wanda Topolska Shanfari

ISBN 978-99969-52-00-5